D1621934

Guitar for Kids
A Beginner's Guide

By Mark Daniels

ISBN-13: 978-1502596796
ISBN-10: 1502596792
Guitar for Kids: A Beginner's Guide

Table of Contents

Hello!

My name is Barry and I am a guitar playing monster. No really. I am a monster who can play a guitar like nobody's business. I have been strumming the old six string for well over 400 years, and I have seen and learned it all.

During those 400 years of becoming one with my guitar, I have picked up some REAL guitar playing secrets and guess what? It is time for me to pass those guitar playing secrets on to you my little guitar playing amigo. That's right. It will be you and me. Human student and Monster teacher.

It doesn't matter if you want to rock the house with your guitar, or if you want to quietly strum a chord or two. What is about to happen is nothing short of FANTASTIC! Your guitar teacher is a monster and that is as cool as it gets. Do any of your friends have a guitar teacher that is a monster? I don't think so.

I won't be the only one teaching you how to play your guitar in this book. My human friend Mark will be helping out a lot. I taught him how to play guitar and he is really good, but I'm better.

Okay, let's make some music!

The Guitar Explained

Take a look at your guitar. Its pretty cool isn't it? I will tell you a little secret that no other guitar teacher knows about. Your guitar wants you to play it. It wants you to pick it up and make some noise with it. If your guitar had a mouth, it would be smiling every time it was in your hands. Go ahead and play around with it. Just make some noise with it. Make your guitar happy!

Do you know what kind of guitar you have? I don't mean the name brand because that doesn't really matter. I am talking about the type of guitar. You might have a really cool ACOUSTIC guitar like this one.

Acoustic Guitar

Or you may have a rocking electric guitar like this one.

Electric Guitar

Both types are cool, but they are both very different guitars. Let's take a closer look at the ACOUSTIC guitar first.

I like to think of my guitar as having three sections or pieces. Kind of like a pizza but without the cheese and pepperoni.

My guitar has a Body, a Neck and a Headstock. So does yours. The next picture should help you understand

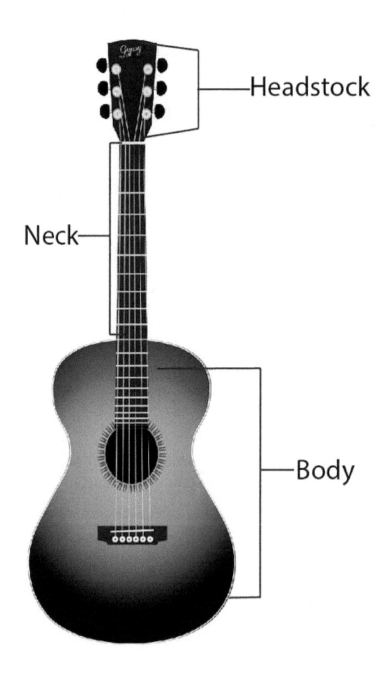

Headstock

Neck

Body

Now let's take a closer look at the Headstock. This is the part of your guitar that lets you keep everything in tune. Don't worry. The headstock on your guitar may look a little different than mine. It's okay because most headstocks do look different from one another.

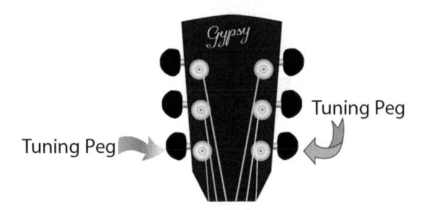

See those shiny knobby looking things? Those are called TUNING PEGS and they are almost like magic because they let you change the pitch of each string on your guitar. You have to be really gentle with these because if you turn them too far in the wrong direction, you will break a string and that is no fun!

Notice how there is one tuning peg for every string on your guitar? That is because each tuning peg controls the pitch of its very own string. See the image below.

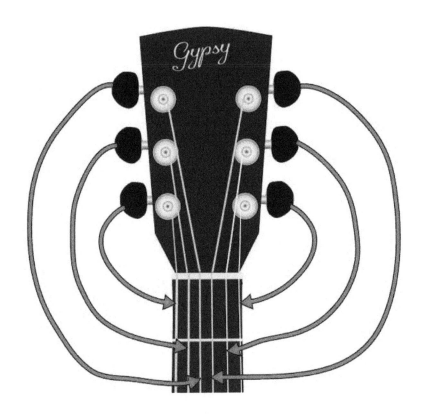

Turning the tuning peg in one direction will tighten the string and make the pitch of the string go higher. Turning the tuning peg in the opposite direction will loosen the string and make the pitch of the string go lower. Don't turn any of these yet.

The next part of the guitar is the long skinny part. This is called the NECK. The neck on your guitar might not look exactly like mine and that is okay.

This is the part of the guitar where your left hand will be playing and dancing. Go ahead and take a closer look at the NECK. Get up close and look at it. Move your hands over the strings.

Does the neck of your guitar have spots like mine does? These help you keep track of where your hand is and where it needs to go when you start playing your guitar. Not all guitar necks have spots. Some of them have squares or rectangles.

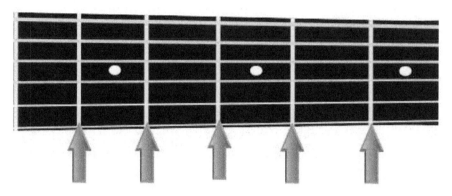

Frets

Do you see those little metal bars all over the neck? Those are called frets. A different note lives between each fret. As you move up the neck towards the BODY of the guitar the notes get higher in pitch. That is how you get those really high pitched notes that have been known to break glass.

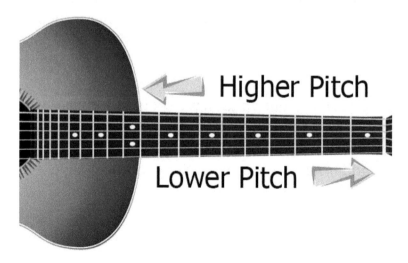

Higher Pitch

Lower Pitch

The part of the neck where your fingers hold down the strings is called the fretboard. This is where the magic happens. This is where your fingers become one with your guitar and beautiful music happens.

The next part of the guitar is the BODY. This is the biggest part of the guitar. Go ahead and look it over. What's the first thing you see? I can't help but notice that giant hole right in the middle.

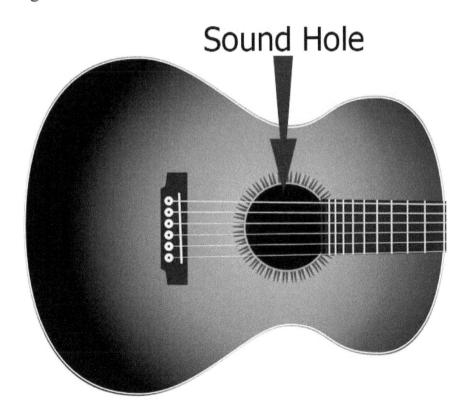

Sound Hole

Don't worry. Your guitar is not broken. It is supposed to have a big hole in the middle of the BODY. This hole is called the sound hole. Let's see if the sound hole is working correctly.

Get as close to the sound hole as you can. Take a peek inside. Hopefully you don't see any little musical gremlins hiding in there. Now comes the fun part. Put your mouth close to the sound hole and yell, scream or sing right into the hole.

Did you notice how your voice sounded different. It sounded bigger didn't it? This means the sound hole on your guitar is working. That hole makes the sound of your strings louder. Without the sound hole, your guitar would be so quiet a mouse couldn't even hear it.

There is one more part on the BODY. It is called the BRIDGE.

Bridge

This is where the strings start on your guitar. You can follow them all the way up the NECK until they reach the tuning pegs on the HEADSTOCK.

Congratulations my guitar playing friend. You now know the three parts to your acoustic guitar.

Now let's take a closer look at an electric guitar. Electric guitars kind of look the same. The NECK and HEADSTOCK are pretty much the same. Look closely though. There is something missing from the body on the electric guitar. Can you guess what it is?

Electric guitars don't have a sound hole, do they? Electric guitars don't need a sound hole because they use an amplifier to make them REALLY LOUD!

You may have also noticed an electric guitar has more stuff on the BODY. What is all of this stuff? Let's take a look!

Pickups

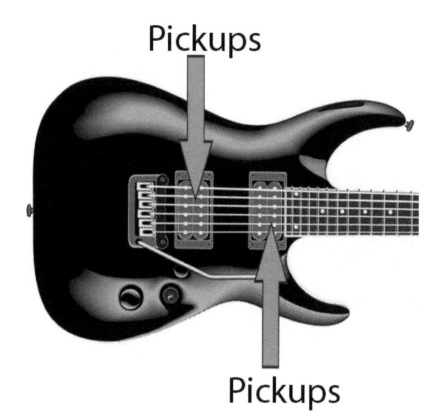

Pickups

These are called pickups. You could think of the pickup as the microphone on your electric guitar. Pickups amplify the sounds of the strings and send the sound to your amplifier. The pickups on your electric guitar may look different. It may only have one pickup, or it might have three.

There is an input jack on your electric guitar too. This is where you plug in the guitar cable. The other end of the guitar cable plugs into an amplifier.

Input Jack

Your guitar may also have some knobs too. The volume knob is the one you need to be careful with. The volume knob lets you crank the volume of your guitar really loud. IT GETS SO LOUD THAT EVERYONE WILL BE SHOUTING AT THE TOP OF THEIR LUNGS. TURN IT DOWN PLEASE!

Now you know the power of an electric guitar. Use it wisely!

How To Hold Your Guitar

Now that you have become one with your guitar, it is time to learn the right way to hold this thing. Are you ready to make your guitar happy?

Let's start by learning how to hold your guitar while sitting down. You can play standing up, but it is easier to learn how to play sitting down. You can sit on a couch, a bed or a chair with no arms. You can even sit on the floor, but it won't be as comfortable.

Relax and get comfortable in your seat, but don't slouch! Slouching is bad for your back and it makes playing your new guitar even harder. Sit up straight and hold your guitar like this.

The back of the guitar should be resting against your stomach. The sound hole should be facing away from you and the thickest string should be on the top. The bent part of the BODY of the guitar should be resting on your leg.

You can also hold your guitar with your legs crossed like this.

The main goal of holding your guitar is comfort. Try to sit as comfortable as possible and holding your guitar will be easy.

Using Your Hands As A Team

Before you jump into rocking the house down, you need to learn where and how you will be using your hands. This part of the book is for people who write with their right hand. If you are left handed, you will need a special "lefty"guitar. Don't worry. I am not going to leave the leftys out. They need to learn how to rock too!

Here is another secret I learned in my 400 years of playing guitar. Your hands will be working together like a team. One hand will be doing all the strumming while the other hand moves and dances all over the neck. It may seem like they are doing different things, but they will actually be working together to make your guitar happy.

Your right hand will be doing all of the strumming down by the sound hole or the pickups. Your right hand has now been magically transformed into your STRUMMING HAND.

Your left hand is important too. Let's make it part of the team. Your left hand will be used to hold down the strings on the fret board. You will only be using four fingers on the fret board. Your thumb will rest on the back of the neck and help you keep your hand steady.

For all of you leftys out there that feel the need to hold a guitar in their hands and make magical music, you will be doing everything the opposite of the right handers out there. Your left hand will be doing all of the strumming down by the sound hole or the pickups. Your left hand will now become your STRUMMING HAND.

Your right hand needs to be part of the team. Your right hand will be dancing and jumping around on the neck of the guitar while your left hand does all of the strumming.

Strumming for the First Time

What? You haven't already strummed your guitar yet? Let's get to it and make some magic happen.

Strumming is easy, but you can do it wrong. Strumming the wrong way could break the strings on your guitar and it will knock your guitar out of tune. Strumming should be nice and easy. Don't pull the strings.

If you are right handed, then forget about your left hand for a minute. Leftys, you need to forget about your right hand for a minute. We are only going to be using our STRUMMING hand.

Let's start by strumming using just the thumb on your strumming hand. Rest the side of your thumb on the thickest string.

Now slowly move your thumb down all of the strings like this. Your thumb should lightly brush against all of the strings and you should hear them loud and clear.

If your thumb gets caught on the strings, keep trying until it moves over the strings nice and smooth. Don't press down on the strings when you strum. Just lightly move your thumb over them.

Strumming your guitar is powerful. You can make your guitar louder by strumming harder. Give it a try, but not too hard. You don't want to break the strings!

Picking for the First Time

Now we can move on to some serious strumming. This time we are going to be using a pick. You do have a guitar pick don't you? Hopefully you have a bunch of them because they are very easy to lose.

If you are playing an acoustic guitar, you may even drop your pick in the sound hole every once in a while. I used to do that all the time. Getting it out of there is easy. I just hold my guitar upside down with the sound hole facing the floor and gently shake it until the pick falls out.

Strumming with a pick is different than strumming with your fingers. A pick gives you more power when you strum and it lets you easily strum just one string at a time if you want. When you get really good at playing guitar, your pick will be moving so fast that you can't even see it.

Here is another little secret you need to know. There is more than one way to hold a pick. People often ask me, "Barry, what is the best way to hold a guitar pick?" My reply is always the same. "The right way to hold a guitar pick is the way that is the most comfortable for you."

This is really important because if you are holding the guitar pick in an uncomfortable way, then your hand will start to hurt and you won't want to play your guitar anymore.

The pointy part of the pick is what we use to strum with. I place my pick on my index finger like the image below.

I hold it lightly between my thumb and index finger like the image below.

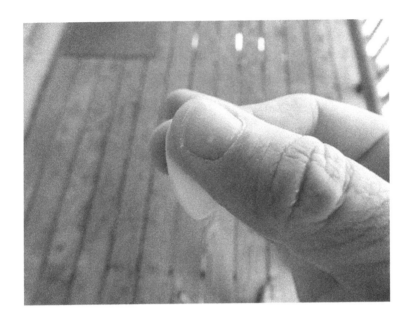

I have found holding the guitar pick like this gives me the most control and comfort. Give it a try and see if it works for you.

Now that you know how to hold the pick, you must learn how to use it as well. Using the pick the wrong way can and will break the strings on your guitar. Do you remember how to strum with your thumb? Using a pick is not much different.

Use the pointy part of the pic to strum the strings. Start at the top string and move your hand down like the images below.

Make sure you hold the pick tight. Don't use the pick to dig into the strings either. The pick should move nice and easy over the strings. This is one area where you will need to practice. The more you practice, the better you will be.

Listening to Your Guitar

Once you start strumming your guitar, you should be able to hear it pretty good. If you have an electric guitar, you won't be able to hear your guitar as well unless you have it plugged into an amplifier.

Here is another secret I learned a long time ago. When you start to get a little more comfortable with your guitar, you can rest your ear on the side while you are playing. Give it a try. It may seem a little awkward at first, but rest your ear on the side of your guitar and strum the strings.

You can hear your guitar loud and clear can't you? Your ears are picking up the vibrations from the guitar strings as they are being carried through the body of the guitar. This is how every guitar works. The neck and the body of the guitar help carry the string vibrations all over the place.

Whenever I need to play really quietly, this is how I do it. It lets me hear everything the guitar is trying to tell me.

This neat trick works for both electric guitars and acoustic guitars.

The Playing Hand

Your playing hand is the hand that will be dancing all over the neck of the guitar. Your four fingers will be used to press the strings against the fretboard. This part can be tricky to master. It may even make the tips of your fingers sore. That's okay. You will need to have tough fingers in order to play guitar like a pro and holding the guitar neck the right way will make your fingers tough.

Your thumb will be used to brace your hand on the back of

the guitar neck like this.

The position of your fingers and your thumb on the back of the neck will change all the time. Do what feels comfortable.

Holding the strings against the fretboard in the right place is very important. If you press the string too close the fret like in the image below, the note won't be clear and crisp. The string may even make a loud buzzing sound. It sounds cool, but it blocks out the sound of the note.

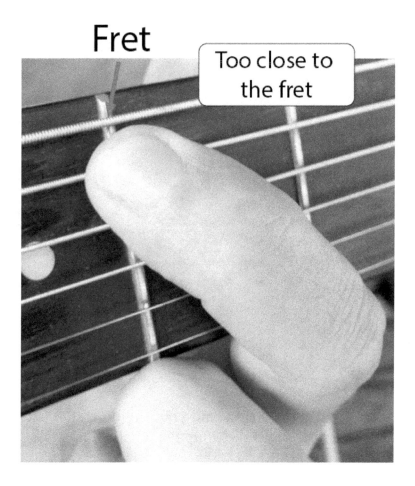

If you press the string too far away from the fret like the picture below, it may be too hard to keep it pressed against the fretboard.

Fret

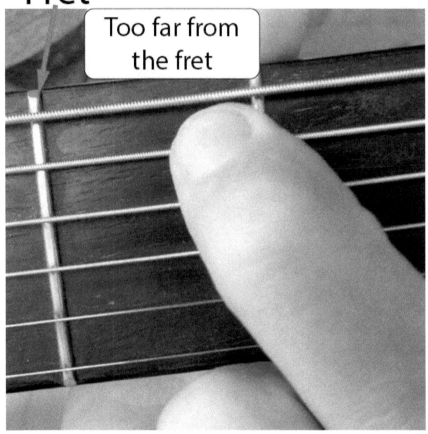

Too far from the fret

Try to keep your finger close to the middle like this.

Practice holding down each string in different places on the neck using different fingers on your playing hand.

Your wrist will constantly be moving and changing as you play. Try to keep your playing hand as relaxed and as comfortable as possible. It will take a little bit of practice getting your playing hand used to this.

This is where your hands finally get to work together. Your playing hand will press a string or strings against the fretboard while your strumming hand strums those strings. It can be a little tricky getting your hands to work together like a team, but practice makes everything easier.

Giving each one of your playing fingers a name makes it easier for me to tell you how to play guitar. Let's use a number because numbers are easier to remember. Your pointer finger will now be called the 1st finger. Your middle finger will now be called your 2nd finger. Your ring finger will now be called your 3rd finger and your pinky finger will now be called your 4th finger. Look at the image below.

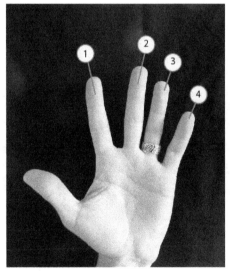

Remember this. You will need it later when we start jamming on your shiny new guitar!

Know Your Strings

Let's take a closer look at the strings on your guitar. There should be six of them. The strings get smaller and thinner from top to bottom. Look at them really close. Each string is a little different isn't it? The string that you rested your thumb on during the strumming lesson is thicker than the rest of them. It also has a lower pitch.

In order to make things easier to understand, the guitar strings have been numbered. The smallest or thinnest string is called the First string. The next string is called the second and then the third, fourth, fifth and finally the sixth. This picture should make it easy to understand.

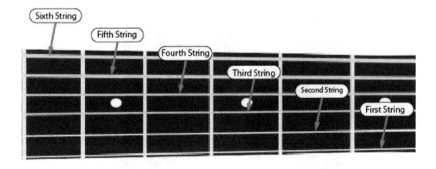

It may seem backwards to call the smallest and last string you see the first, but that is just the way it is. Remember, the smallest string is the FIRST string.

Using your pick or your thumb, lightly pluck the thickest or SIXTH string. Listen to it. It sounds pretty cool doesn't it? Believe it or not, you just made music. Congratulations!

When you pluck a string without your playing hand pressing it down anywhere on the neck of your guitar, this is called playing an OPEN string. It is open because your fingers are not holding it down on the fretboard.

Use the palm of your hand to mute the strings. Just rest your hand on the strings like this.

Notice how the sound stops? This is a quick and easy way to keep your guitar quiet.

Move your thumb or pick over the next string or the FIFTH string and lightly pluck it. You just made music again! Notice how this string is higher in pitch? Use the palm of your hand to mute the strings again.

Use your pick or your thumb to lightly pluck each string and listen to the way they sound. As you work your way down the strings pay close attention to the sound. They should get higher in pitch.

Each string also sings a musical note when played open.

The SIXTH string is a low E note.
The FIFTH string is an A note.
The FOUR string is a D note.
The THIRD string is a G note.
The SECOND string is a B note.
The FIRST string is a high E note.

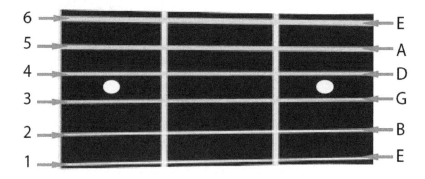

Did you notice how the SIXTH string and the FIRST string are both E notes, but they sound totally different? Try this little trick with your strumming hand. Rest your thumb on the top side of the SIXTH or LOW E string and rest your pointing finger on the bottom of the FIRST or HIGH E string like this.

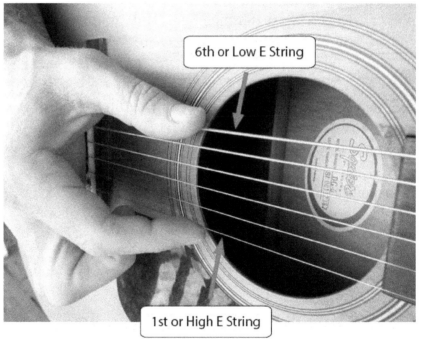

6th or Low E String

1st or High E String

Now try to pluck both open strings at the same time. Don't pull the strings. Don't push them. Just let the sides of your fingers lightly brush against them. If your guitar is tuned, both notes should blend together nicely. It sounds really cool.

Low Notes VS High Notes

Knowing the difference between low notes and high notes can be tricky at first, but it gets easier the more you play your guitar.

The words low and high don't refer to the volume of your guitar. There is a big difference here. Low volume would be a tiny little whisper. HIGH VOLUME WOULD BE SOMEONE SHOUTING!

Low pitch is the LOW E or SIXTH string on your guitar. A higher pitch note would be the HIGH E or FIRST string of your guitar.

Here is another awesome secret. The notes get higher in pitch as you work your way up the neck or towards the sound hole of your guitar. Let's give it a try.

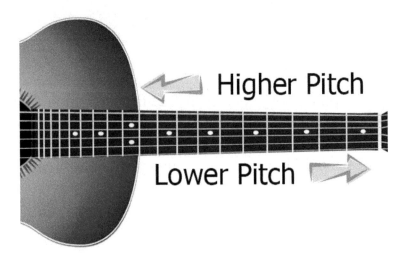

Use your pick or your thumb to strum the SIXTH or LOW E string on the guitar. Go ahead strum just that one note. Listen to it. Now mute the string with the palm of your strumming hand by lightly resting your hand on the string.

Use your 1st or index finger to press down the FIFTH string on the second fret. Remember to keep your finger as close to the middle of the frets as possible.

Now strum the same string with your pick or your thumb.

Move your first finger up to the next empty space and try again. Now move your finger up to the next empty space and try again. Did you notice how the pitch gets higher every time you move your 1st finger higher up the neck? This is the difference in low pitch notes and high pitch notes.

Try this same thing on every string and notice how the sound changes. Now you are really making music. Good job. Practice with different playing fingers on the neck. You need to get every finger used to pressing down the strings on the fretboard, even your little pinky or 4th finger.

Tuning Your Guitar With A Tuner

You know what they say. You can tune a guitar, but you can't tuna fish. Ha ha! Tuning your guitar can be tough because there is so much to learn. You must know what note each string should be and you need to know which direction to turn the tuning peg on the headstock.

If your parents aren't already helping you with this book and your guitar, then go get them. Tell them Barry the monster says they need to help you tune your guitar.

Did you get your parents? Are they sitting there reading this with you? Well good. Let me introduce myself then.

Hi parents. My name is Barry and I am a guitar playing monster. It is time to learn how to tune a guitar. Help your child with this part. Most kids are not ready to learn how to tune a guitar when they first start playing.

It takes a little while to understand when a guitar is in or out of tune. If the guitar is not in tune, it won't sound too good. Learning how to tune a guitar is very important and easy if you follow these instructions.

You will need an electronic tuner to make this easier. I highly recommend a clip on tuner. The tuner I am going to be using for this example is the Fender FT-004. At the time of this writing, this tuner was less than $10.00 at Amazon.

You can get one at the link below. It even comes with a battery.

http://www.amazon.com/Fender-FT-004-Chromatic-Clip-On-Tuner/dp/B005MR6IHK/

First, let's look at this little gadget.

Front View of Tuner

Side View of Tuner

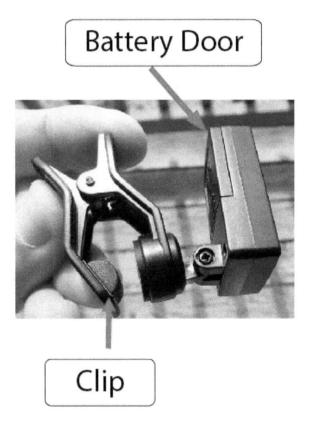

Battery Door

Clip

The really cool thing about this tuner is this. It feels the vibrations of your guitar to help you tune it perfectly. It's almost like magic! This tuner also works with a ukelele, violin, cello or bass guitar.

This tuner is called a clip on tuner because it easily clips on to the headstock of your guitar like this.

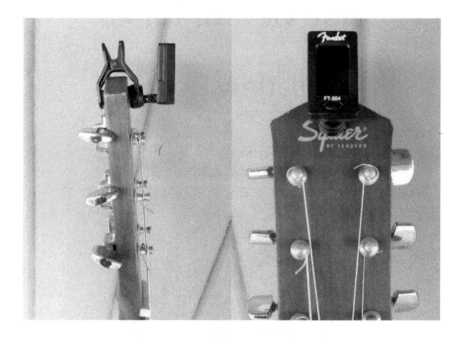

Now let's take a closer look at the digital display. This is where all the magic will be happening.

Tuning Arrow

String Note

String Number   Current Tuning Mode

There is a lot of stuff on the screen of your tuner isn't
there, but this little device makes it SO much easier to
perfectly tune your guitar. The example image shows the
1ST STRING or HIGH E string in perfect tune!

The little 1 in the bottom left of the display tells you which
string you are trying to tune. In this example, it is the
FIRST STRING. The G in the bottom right of the display
tells you which mode is currently selected. In this example,
we are tuning a Guitar. G stands for Guitar.

If your tuner doesn't show a G in the bottom right corner of the display, then lightly press the power mode button. If you hold this button in, the tuner will shut off. If you press the button quickly, you will change tuning modes. Simple and easy! Press it to change the mode until it shows a letter G in the bottom right corner of the display.

The GIANT E in the middle of the display tells you which note the string is supposed to be. If the note is out of tune, the screen will be blue. The screen changes to green once the string is in tune.

The tuning arrow will help guide you. It will tell you if the pitch of the current string is too low or too high. If the arrow is on the left side of the display, the pitch is too low. If the arrow is on the right side of the display, the pitch is too high. When the arrow is in the middle of the display, the pitch is perfect! Here are some good examples.

Tuning arrow is on the left side of the display.

The pitch is too low!

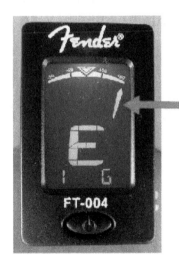

Tuning arrow is on the right side of the display.

The pitch is too high!

Tuning arrow is in the middle of the display.

The pitch is perfect.
This string is in tune.

All right! Now that you know how the tuner works, let's put everything you just learned into action. It's time to tune your guitar and with the help of your tuner, it will be simple!
Let's start on the LOW E string or SIXTH STRING.

It may be easier for you to lay your guitar on your lap. This way you can easily see the tuner, strum the guitar string and turn the tuning peg at the same time.

Make sure your tuner is clipped to the headstock of your guitar, the power is on and the tuner is in GUITAR mode. There should be a G in the lower right corner of the display.

G for guitar mode.

Strum the LOW E or SIXTH string of your guitar. Try to strum the string lightly at first to see how the tuner responds to it. You may need to keep strumming it to get the best response from the tuner.

In this example, the pitch of the LOW E or SIXTH STRING is too low. Notice how the tuning arrow is on the left side of the display screen?

Tuning arrow on the far left means pitch is too low.

In the music world, when the pitch is too low, it is called FLAT. You must make the pitch higher. To make the pitch higher on my guitar, I turn the tuning peg counter clockwise like in the image below.

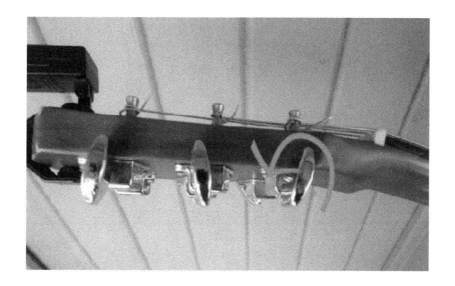

Keep slowly turning the tuning peg until the tuning arrow on the display screen reaches the middle like the picture below.

Now the LOW E or SIXTH STRING is perfectly tuned!
Let's tune the next string.

The next string is the A or FIFTH STRING. In this
example the pitch is too high. Notice how the tuning arrow
is on the right side of the display screen?

Tuning arrow on the far
right means pitch is too high.

To make the pitch lower on my guitar, I turn the tuning peg
clockwise like in the image below.

Keep slowly turning the tuning peg until the tuning arrow
on the display screen reaches the middle like the picture
below.

Now all you need to do is repeat this process for the rest of the strings on your guitar.

The 4th string should be tuned to D.
The 3rd string should be tuned to G.
The 2nd string should be tuned to B.
The 1st string should be tuned to E.

When you are done, go back and make sure all of the strings stayed in tune. Sometimes they will come out of tune when you are tuning other strings.

Tuning Your Guitar With A Piano or Electronic Keyboard

You don't have to use a tuner to tune your guitar. You can always tune your guitar using a piano or a keyboard. This method of tuning your guitar is a little harder than using an electronic tuner because you have to match the pitch of your guitar to the pitch of your piano.

First you will need to locate the notes on the piano. Use this handy image below.

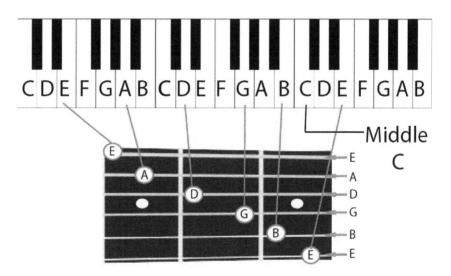

There is a lot of stuff going on up there in that picture, but if you look closely you will see that each string matches a key on the piano. You will need to listen to the notes on your guitar and compare them to the notes on your piano and change the notes on your guitar until they sound just like the notes on the piano. With a little practice, you will get it down in no time.

Chords

Anytime you play more than two notes at the same time on your guitar, you are playing a chord. You can even make up your own chords if you want, but there are a few chords that every guitar player should learn how to play.

Playing chords will require some practice on your part, but the more you practice, the better you will be at playing your guitar. I will give you plenty of great picture examples to make it easy to understand where your playing fingers should be and which strings you should be strumming. You will also learn how to read chord charts. Let's get ready to make some music!

Chord Charts Explained

Take a look at the chord chart below.

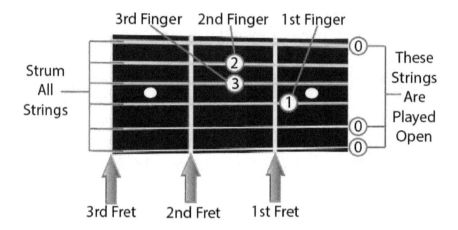

Wow! There is a lot of stuff going on in that chord chart isn't there? Chord charts are pretty easy to understand though. On the left side of the chord chart it tells you which strings to strum. In this example, you would be strumming every string on the guitar.

The bottom of the chord chart tells you where the chord is played on the neck of the guitar. In this example, the chord is played on the 1st and 2nd frets.

The right side of the chord chart tells you which strings should be played open. Do you remember what it means to play an open string? It means you DO NOT press the string down on the fretboard.

You may have also noticed some circles with numbers in the middle on the fretboard. Do you remember when we gave each finger on your playing hand a number?

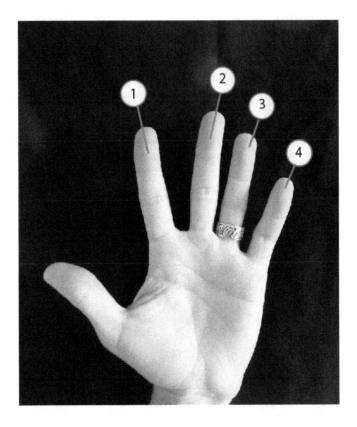

These numbers on the chord chart represent which playing finger should be holding the string down on the fretboard.

For each chord explanation, I will show you a chord chart and a real life picture to help you understand exactly how to play the chord. You will be rocking in no time. Let's look at our first chord.

The E Major Chord

This is the chord chart for the E Major chord. All strings are being strummed and you will be using 3 fingers on the fretboard.

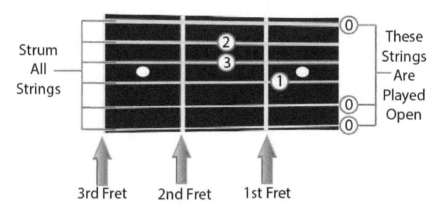

3rd Fret   2nd Fret   1st Fret

This is what the E Major chord looks like on the guitar neck.

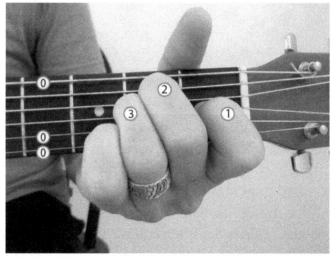

Here is a side view of the E Major chord on the guitar neck. Notice how the 4th finger is not pressing any strings on the fretboard?

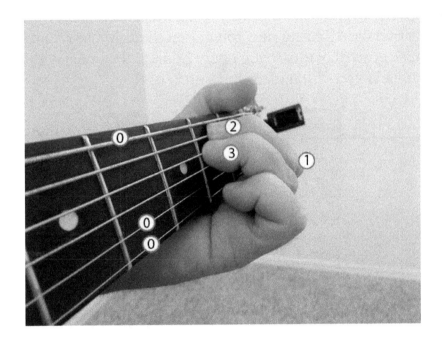

The E Minor Chord

The E Minor chord is almost exactly like the E Major chord. Only one note is different. You don't use your 1st finger on the 4th string like you did on the E Major chord. Instead, you play this string open. Look at the images below and you will understand.

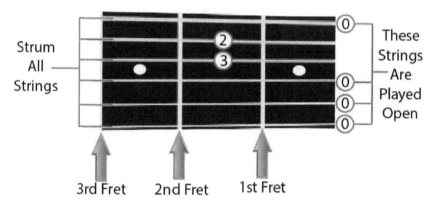

This is what the E Minor chord looks like on the guitar neck.

Here is another view of the E Minor chord.

The A Major Chord

There is more than one way to play the A Major chord. Here is the easiest way to play it. You will be using your 1st finger, your 2nd finger and your 3rd finger to hold the strings down. You do not strum the SIXTH or LOW E string on this chord.

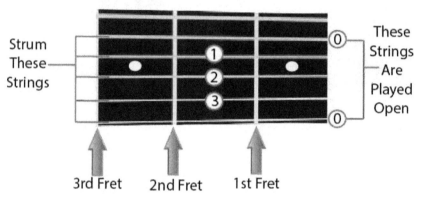

Strum These Strings

These Strings Are Played Open

3rd Fret   2nd Fret   1st Fret

This is what the A Major chord looks like on the guitar neck. Do not strum the SIXTH or LOW E string.

Here is another way to play the A Major chord. This way is a little harder because you have to press three strings against the fretboard using only one finger like this.

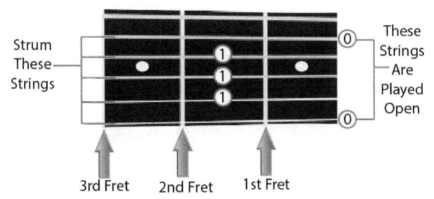

Strum These Strings

These Strings Are Played Open

3rd Fret   2nd Fret   1st Fret

This is what the other way to play the A Major chord looks like on the guitar neck.

Can you see how you use only one finger to hold down three strings? This way is difficult to master and it can make your finger sore.

The A Minor Chord

The A Minor chord is a lot like the E Major chord. Your playing fingers will be in the same position, but on different strings. Look at the chord chart below.

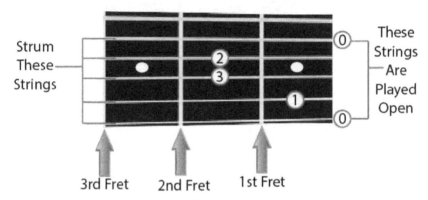

This is what the A Minor chord looks like on the guitar neck.

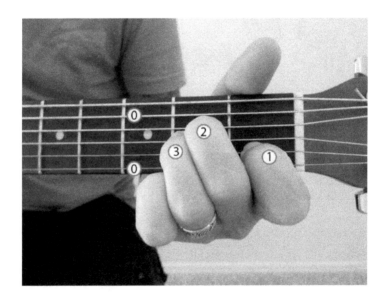

Here is another view of the A Minor chord.

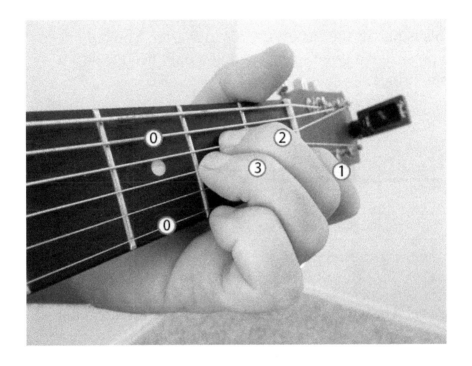

The D Major Chord

This is one of the easiest chords to master. You only need to press down three strings and you only need to strum four strings.

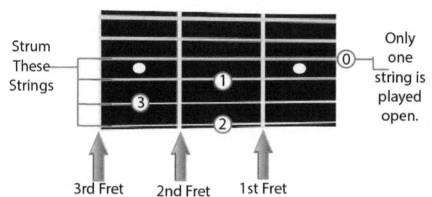

This is what the D Major chord looks like on the guitar neck.

Here is another view of the D Major chord.

The D Minor Chord

Have you noticed how these chords have two versions? A Major and a Minor. If you listen closely, you can easily hear the difference in each chord. Major chords always sound happy. Minor chords always sound sad. Here is how you play a D Minor chord.

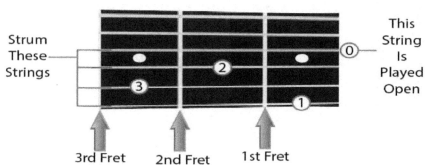

Strum These Strings

This String Is Played Open

3rd Fret   2nd Fret   1st Fret

This is what the D Minor chord looks like on the guitar neck.

The C Major Chord

The C Major chord can be hard to master because you really need to stretch your fingers without muting the open strings. Look at the chord chart below.

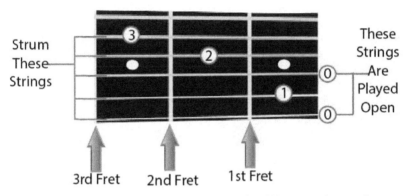

This is what the C Major chord looks like on the guitar neck.

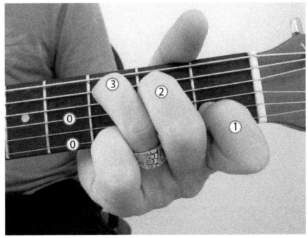

Here is another view of the C Major chord.

The G Chord

The G chord sounds so nice. It uses all the strings and when your guitar is in perfect tune, this chord really sounds great.

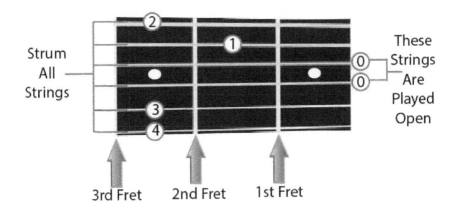

This is what the G chord looks like on the guitar neck.

Here is another view of the G chord.

The Mighty Power Chord Version 1

This is the chord that helped shape rock and roll music. It is only two notes, but it sounds really powerful. This chord really sounds best on an electric guitar, but it works well on an acoustic guitar too. The coolest thing about this chord is the fact that it can be played anywhere on the guitar neck. You can move it anywhere on the neck and it still sounds good. This chord is also the easiest to master!

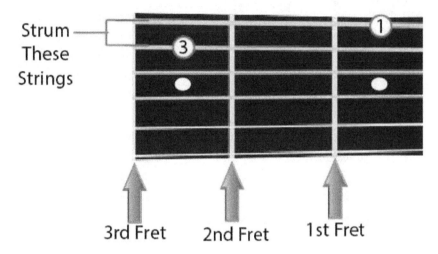

Strum
These
Strings

3rd Fret   2nd Fret   1st Fret

This is what the Power chord looks like on the guitar neck.

Here is another view of the Power chord.

Here is the really neat thing about this chord. You can move it around the neck of the guitar and you can move it to different strings. Instead of playing the power chord on the SIXTH and FIFTH strings like we did in the example above, let's try playing it on the FIFTH and FOURTH strings. Here is an example.

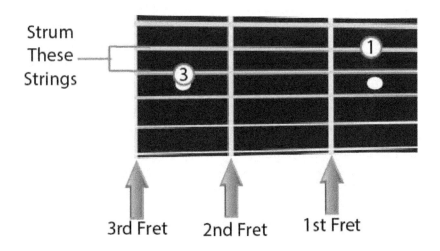

Strum These Strings

3rd Fret   2nd Fret   1st Fret

This is what the Power chord looks like on the guitar neck.

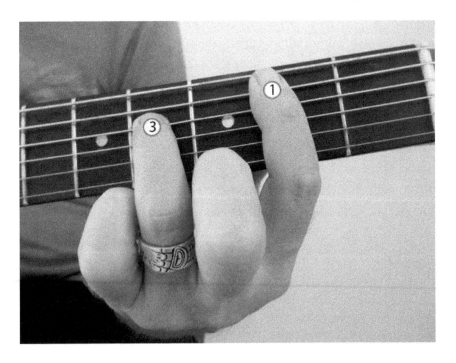

Here is another view of the same power chord.

This time we will play the power chord on the THIRD and FOURTH strings like this.

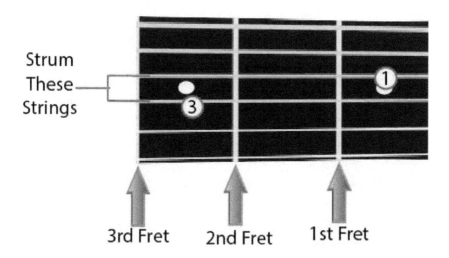

This is what the Power chord looks like on the guitar neck.

Here is another view of the same power chord.

The Super Power Chord

All right, now that you have that power chord mastered, let's make it a little better. Let's add one more note to this chord to make it even more powerful. Let's try it on the first power chord we learned. This time we will be holding down one more note with our 4th finger like the chart below.

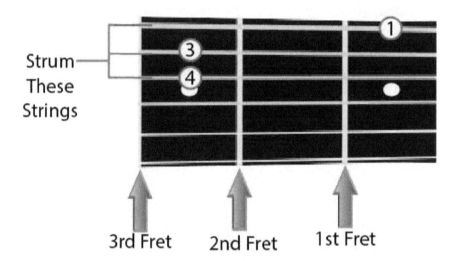

This is what the super power chord looks like on the guitar neck.

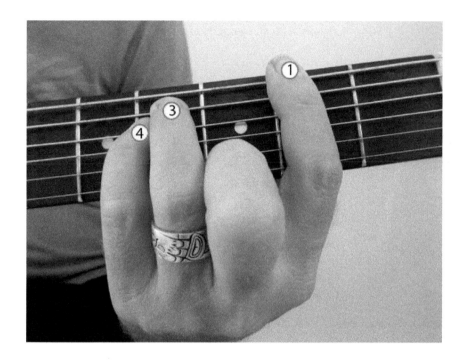

Here is another view of the same power chord.

You can move this chord all over the guitar neck too. Let's try it on the next three strings.

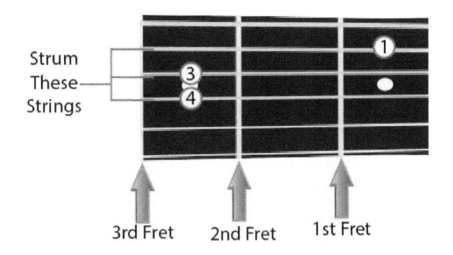

Strum
These
Strings

3rd Fret   2nd Fret   1st Fret

This is what the super power chord looks like on the guitar neck.

Here is another view of the same power chord.

You can move this chord all over the guitar neck too! You can also move down to the next set of strings, but this time it is a little different. Your 4th finger will need to move up one fret. Look at the chord chart below.

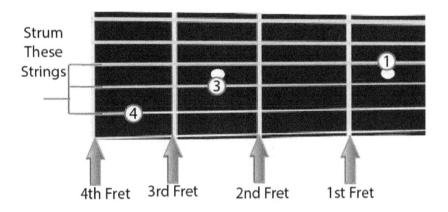

Strum These Strings

4th Fret   3rd Fret   2nd Fret   1st Fret

This is what the super power chord looks like on the guitar neck.

Here is another view of the same power chord.

Practice Makes Perfect

Congratulations! You have made it to the end of the book, but this is just the beginning for you! It is now up to you to practice everything you learned. Practice those chords and start playing them one after another. Mix them all up. That's how you make your own music!

The more you practice, the better you will get. Playing your guitar may seem hard at first. That's okay. I know mine was really hard to play when I first started playing, but I noticed that each day I practiced, I got better. Now I no longer practice my guitar. I just play it.

There may be days when you look at your guitar and think to yourself, "I don't feel like practicing." That's okay too. We all have days when we just don't want to pick up the guitar and make it happy. But remember this, you can't get better at playing guitar without practicing. Try to practice at least 10 minutes a day.

Thanks!

Thanks for reading my book! I really appreciate it and I hope you learned a lot. If you enjoyed Guitar for Kids: A Beginner's Guide, then leave a review. I would really appreciate it.

I am currently in the process of writing several more great guitar playing books. If you want to be the first to find out about any new books that I publish and get them for FREE, then sign up to my **new book release** email list.

I promise not to share your email address with anyone, and I won't send you tons of junk mail. (I will only contact you when a new book is out.)

Use this link to sign up!

http://eepurl.com/4ITh9

CPSIA information can be obtained
at www.ICGtesting.com
Printed in the USA
LVHW081005271018
594253LV00007B/13/P